Christianity in the Midst of an *Emotionalist Society*

Domingo González Jr.

CHRISTIANITY IN THE MIDST OF AN EMOTIONALIST SOCIETY

First edition. November 18, 2023.

ISBN: 979-8223781974

Written by Domingo González Jr..

Also by Domingo González Jr.

Cristianismo en Medio De una Sociedad Emocionalista
Christianity in the Midst of an Emotionalist Society
Cristianismo No Meio de uma Sciedade Emocionalista

Christianity in the midst of an Emotionalist Society.

Cover Designed from images generated on:
https://stablediffusionweb.com/ and edited on: https://pinetools.com/
es

Domingo González Jr.

2023

DEDICATION

I love the church of Christ and I suffer to see how it is deceived and manipulated. I dedicate this book to every man, woman and child who considers himself a child of God and who truly wants to be a church.

This book is dedicated to each one of you, with all the love that can come from me.

THANKS

I thank God for opening my eyes and making me see all the emotional manipulations in the church and for giving me enough fear not to be part of this practice.

The first person who taught me how to detect emotional manipulations in the church was my mother, although she would end up using those tools too, but I would be ungrateful if I didn't thank her for that.

I thank God for Juan Manuel Vaz, Paul Washer, Sugel Michelen and Miguel Núñez, because their well-focused positions on this topic were very helpful to me.

CONTENT

INTRODUCTION

Unfortunately, we live in a society where emotions and feelings govern all areas, even in government.

We have people who, regardless of their genetics, regardless of whether their genes say they are men, if they "feel" like women, they must be treated as women. And if that were all, there would be no problem, but laws are also enacted to defend your rights and to make matters worse, laws are enacted to force others to support your perception.

We live in a society where it is not the truth that matters, but how the truth that was told to me made me feel.

This society is full of what they call "the crystal generation" because of how emotionally delicate people are. Nowadays it is almost impossible to say something or give an opinion without someone being offended, no matter how delicately we try so that this "glass generation" is not offended.

It should be noted that this name "glass generation" has nothing to do with age, there are 15-year-old boys who belong to this generation as well as 60-year-old boys.

People without formed character, incapable of accepting correction or advice because they brand the counselor or the person who corrects them as "abusive" or "insensitive" without empathy.

And although all of this is actually a big problem, there have always been people who have benefited from these. How? Well, becoming experts in manipulating people's emotions.

And don't believe, this is not something new, one of the most evil people who ever existed, Adolf Hitler, already took advantage of this, he managed to convince an entire nation that his atrocities were correct. It is said that the secret of his great speeches was his emotional ability.

For hundreds of years great tyrants have used emotional manipulation to make people feel what they want them to feel and even to make them think what they want them to think.

It wouldn't be too big a problem if this had stayed outside the church doors.

The big problem with this is that it penetrated the doors of the churches and today there are people considered as "men of God" who are manipulators of emotions. They play with people's emotions to the point of making them believe what they want them to believe even when the Bible says the opposite.

This should sound the alarm bells in Zion, but Zion sleeps, and while the church slept, the devil planted all this and the problem is that he continues to sleep.

After writing my third book, "A Different Kind of Glory", I said to myself "My idea is not to write a thousand books, only those that I consider can be of great blessing to the church and with those three that is fine."

But then I remembered something that happened in the church where I come from, where a young musician who had just arrived at the church from another congregation, told me "I don't need to pray a lot to make people cry while I lead praise, just say the words." right words at the right time" (More about this story in my book "Skeletons in the Closet: Memoirs of a Pastor's Son)

Well, a few days later this young man became a member of the church and they asked him to lead praise in a Sunday service and I saw how this boy really did just as he told me, the right words at the right time and he made the whole church to cry without needing the Holy Spirit or anything.

And the last straw is that apart from me (perhaps because he had already told me) no one noticed it, not even the pastors, more right or wrong, it was quite the opposite, they began to praise that boy for his Spirituality. .

I remember trying to warn some brother and they accused me of being jealous of him.

When I remembered all that, which you can read in more detail in my book "Skeletons in the Closet," I realized that perhaps I should write one more book, because the truth was that it was not just that experience with manipulative people that I lived, but that I have so many direct lived experiences that I think I have enough authority to talk about this.

I hope that this book can be a blessing to you and I pray that God opens the eyes of everyone's understanding so that they can correctly understand what I want to convey in this book because every extreme is bad and emotions are not bad as we will see later.

Well, God made us with them, Jesus demonstrated that he had them, but today discernment is super necessary. In these times we have many pseudo worshipers who are considered great worshipers and in reality are great manipulators of emotions, we have many heretics with mega churches who are only good orators, like Hitler was.

Here is my offering of unleavened bread for the people of God so that the eyes of the blind and the ears of the deaf may be opened.

CHAPTER 1

Basic concepts.

I am not one of those who likes to give many definitions or concepts, but it is impossible to start a topic like this without being clear about the basic concepts, so I will try to explain them in a simple, easy and direct way.

I want it to be understood that I cannot and do not want to write in the technical and professional way as John MacArthur writes or as R. C. Sproul or any of them wrote, I do not feel comfortable doing it, ¡I do not feel myself doing it! I have fought so hard to stay a Sunday man and I am not going to back down now because I lose some readers.

Well, to the point.

Emotions

Emotion is the immediate reaction of our body to an external agent. It appears instantly in front of the event and has a short duration.

It is very important to have emotions well defined and valued rationally, since, based on them, feelings regarding the events experienced are born.

For example, if you have just been given the news that you have found the job you longed for, the initial emotion will be surprise and shock. Although it is something you wanted with all your might, you didn't know if you were going to achieve it.

Your brain assimilates this surprise and, as it is something that you have been associating for so long with something positive, feelings such as euphoria, joy, optimism or hope, among others, occur.

What are the main feelings of the human being?

- Love
- The sadness
- The euphoria
- The admiration
- The envy

- The hope
- The anger
- Impatience
- The concern
- The satisfaction
- Gratitude

Sanarai.com

Emotional Intelligence

Daniel Goleman explains that Emotional Intelligence is the set of skills that serve to express and control feelings in the most appropriate way in the personal and social field.

Basic and characteristic characteristics of the emotionally intelligent person:

- Possess a sufficient degree of self-esteem.
- Be positive people
- Know how to give and receive
- Empathy (understanding the feelings of others)
- Recognize your own feelings
- Being able to express positive and negative feelings
- Also be able to control these feelings
- Motivation, enthusiasm, interest
- Have alternative values
- Overcoming difficulties and frustrations
- Find balance between demand and tolerance.

https://www.psicoactiva.com/

What are feelings?

Feelings are a state of mind that occurs in relation to external inputs, considered the mental expression of emotion. Where do feelings come from? When the emotion is processed in the brain and the person is aware of said emotion and the mood it produces, it gives rise to the feeling, therefore the origin of the feelings are the emotions defined and rationally valued that will determine our mood. .

Feeling and emotion: difference

Although both emotions and feelings are the result of an irrational process due to the subjective way of perceiving a given situation, emotions maintain a basic and primitive unidirectional pattern, that is, the emotion appears immediately and spontaneously after the presentation of the stimulus. On the contrary, reflective processes intervene in feelings, in which the person becomes aware of their state of mind and what it is that they are feeling, allowing them to be valued. Once we understand the difference between emotions and feelings, we are going to focus exclusively on feelings.

Feelings: examples

Let's now look at some examples of very frequent feelings that can appear in our daily lives:

We receive an email where our boss tells us that we must go to work on Saturday.

First of all, we may experience an emotion of anger, but after becoming aware of what we are feeling, feelings of sadness for not being able to do what you had planned with your partner or anger for having to go to work on a weekend may appear. .

We find out that two of our friends have been invited to a party to which we have not been invited. First, emotional responses of indignation may appear, but after understanding the situation, feelings of vulnerability may appear, where we feel insecure and wonder why we have not been invited.

They notify us that they are going to promote us at work. For example, it could be that our expressed emotion is not what is expected, reacting with a rather apathetic tone. By processing the news and understanding how we feel, we can be aware of the feeling that comes from us, which can be a feeling of stress and fear, in the face of the challenge that is posed to us.

Marta Thomen Bastards. https://www.psicologia-online.com/

Emotionalist

Person who prioritizes emotions over reason.

In short, an emotion is an instantaneous reaction that, depending on the person, can cause reactions and can produce a certain type of feeling. Emotions are immediate* feelings are produced by emotions when processed.

All the concepts that we saw in this first chapter will be necessary to understand everything that we will see below and will be basic when analyzing the characteristics of a potential victim of an emotional manipulator, but we go one step at a time.

CHAPTER 2
Are Emotions Bad?

In general, the term bad emotions does not exist, but we could all agree, even without investigating too much, that anger, hatred, envy, among others, are negative emotions, but let us remember that our focus is towards Christianity, if I go so far as to say that emotions are not bad, I will not be referring to negative emotions.

I remember that many years ago, due to the much psychological damage I had received, I decided to be a cold person and not show affection towards anyone. After a couple of weeks I realized that it was impossible. We were born with emotions, God created us with emotions, The Bible shows that God has emotions, he got angry several times with the people of Israel and was happy.

Jesus also showed emotions, at one point he was so upset that he beat those who were doing business in the temple with belts (Luke 19:45,46), at another time "he was shaken in spirit and was moved" (John 11:33). , he was glad (Luke 10:21) when he was about to be handed over he felt very sad (Matthew 26:38)

Even the Holy Spirit has emotions, the Bible says that we should not make the Holy Spirit sad (Ephesians 4:30)

Emotions are not bad. Even in the medium that the Holy Spirit uses to deal with us. He rebukes us in our hearts, makes us sad for our wickedness so that we may repent and be reconciled to God.

There are Christian currents that make it seem as if emotions are bad, but that is not the case in any way. There are churches where you cannot applaud or give glory to God, much less raise your voice to praise God because they consider it emotionalism. Not at all! Many consider that our praise manual is the book of psalms and there we find quotes such as the following:

Psalms 33:3: Sing a new song to him: do it well, ringing for joy.

Psalms 32:11: You people of God, praise him and celebrate! And you, who are sincere in heart, sing to God with joy!

Psalms 47:1: Clap your hands happily, people of the world! Praise God with joy!

Psalms 63:5 I will praise you with my lips and shout for joy! That will satisfy me more than the most delicious food!

Psalms 81.1: Let out shouts of praise to God! He is our strength! Sing full of joy to the God of Israel!

Psalms 95:1: Let us sing to God with joy Come on, let us sing with joy!

Psalms 100:1,2: Sing joyfully to God, inhabitants of the whole earth. Serve Jehovah with joy; Come into his presence with rejoicing.

Psalms 107:22 Let us give him tokens of gratitude, and let us present offerings to him! Let us announce with shouts of joy the wonders that he has done!

Psalms 150:3-5: Praise him with the sound of a trumpet; Praise him with psaltery and harp. Praise him with tambourine and dance; Praise him with strings and flutes. praise him with resounding cymbals; Praise him with cymbals of joy.

Regarding praise in heaven we find these verses:

Isaiah 6:1-3: I, Isaiah, saw God sitting on a very high throne, and the temple was covered under his cloak. This happened to me in the year that King Oziah died. I also saw some seraphim flying above God. Each one had six wings: with two wings they flew, with two others they covered their faces, and with the other two they covered themselves from the waist down. With a loud voice they said to each other: "Holy, holy, holy is the only God of Israel, the God of the universe; The whole earth is full of his power! »

Revelation 19:1,5,6: 1 After this I heard a loud voice from a great multitude in heaven, saying, Hallelujah! Salvation and honor and glory and power belong to the Lord our God; 5 And a voice came from the throne saying: Praise our God, all his servants and those who fear him, both small and great. And I heard like the voice of a great multitude, like the roar of many waters, and like the voice of great thunder, saying, Hallelujah, for the Lord our God Almighty reigns!

So where is the problem?

The problem is emotionalism and in the first chapter we agreed that an Emotionalist person prioritizes emotions over reason. The Bible commands us to use reason when worshiping Him (John 4:24)

If a person shouts amen without understanding or analyzing or verifying if what is being said is correct according to the Bible, that person is an Emotionalist.

We must understand that whether it is Paul Washer who is preaching, or MacArthur or whoever we consider to be the most "stupid" of preachers, all teaching must pass through the exhaustive filter of the scriptures, that is, everything in its correct context. This is what our Berean brothers did and they are praised in the scriptures for it (Acts 17:11)

I want to pause for a moment on what I said about the correct context, because nowadays it is fashionable to take isolated verses to make the Bible say what we want it to say. I have realized that even the most heretical pastors give biblical verses, but when you study them in their correct context you realize that never in life does the passage say what they want us to say.

But today the brothers who do like the Berean brothers see them as rebels.

I always remember my mother when I think about this topic. My father was the pastor and obviously his husband and I used to sit next to my mother and while my father preached she made me have a Bible dictionary and several versions of the Bible with me and while my father preached she verified each verse that my father gave. father to see if the teaching her husband was giving was in accordance with the scriptures.

You can imagine that several times my father was upset, but we must understand the importance of this, because perhaps we do not understand it, but in a sermon our eternal life may be at stake.

There are people who, if the pastor injects a sufficient emotional charge while he preaches, forget the Bible and there we would be making one of the most important errors, prioritizing emotions over reason.

There are churches where if you shout while you preach it means you have authority from God, it means you are in the "spirit" therefore, without verifying what you are saying in the scriptures, they take it as truth and shout Amen!

It is not being cold, it is not being apathetic, it is not eliminating emotions, it is "Not prioritizing emotions over words."

Once it happened to me that I was at a sermon and everyone was shouting Amen! But there was a part that didn't add up to me and I went and checked and after I checked and realized it was biblically correct, then I also shouted AMEN.

I remember a brother from a specific denomination who came to visit us and in the service, he did not worship, he did not pray, he just looked around analyzing everything and in the end he left me with a sister a list with suggestions on how I should lead the group. I said to myself "What? I didn't even think he was a Christian! He did not worship, he did not pray because he was not an Emotionalist. I believe that he was not an Emotionalist nor was he a Christian. Beloved, we must flee from both extremes.

One of the great theologians and man of God in history, also recognized as one of God's generals, John Wesley left these recommendations regarding praise in which you will realize that there is no suppression of emotions. I love how point 3 sets the balance for point 2, let's see:

Directions for Congregational Singing

To make this part of worship more acceptable to God and of greater benefit to you and others, be careful to observe the following instructions:

1. Everyone sing. Try to meet with the congregation as frequently as possible. Don't let a little weakness or tiredness stop you. If such a thing is a cross to you, take it up, and you will find it to be a blessing.

2. Sing loudly and vigorously. Don't sing as if you were half dead or half asleep. Raise your voice loudly. Be no more afraid to hear your voice, nor more ashamed to be heard now, than when you sang the songs of Satan.

3. Sing modestly. Do not shout, as if you want to stand out or distinguish yourself from the rest of the congregation, so as not to destroy the harmony. Everyone should try to join their voices with those of the rest of the congregation to produce a clear and melodious sound.

4. Sing on time. Whatever the time in which it is sung, try to keep it, do not get ahead or behind; Follow the guiding voices and go with their time as much as possible. Don't sing too slowly. Dragging time is a natural thing for lazy people and it is time for that habit to disappear from among us and for us to sing all our hymns just as we sang them at the beginning.

5. Above all, sing spiritually. Think of God in every word you sing. May your intention be to please him before yourself or any other creature. To achieve this, pay close attention to the meaning of what you sing and take care that your heart does not become too involved with the melody, but offer it to God continually, so that your singing may be such that the Lord can approve it here.

I think I have already made things clear and I do not want to repeat the same thing, so I am going to end this chapter with two sentences, one sentence from Miguel Núñez and the other from Donald Carson:

"In praising God, we have confused hubbub with joy, and stiffness with reverence."

Miguel Nunez

We must escape from these two extremes: That of an emotional Christianity lacking doctrine and that of a cold orthodoxy lacking emotion.

Donald Carson

CHAPTER 3
An Emotionalist Society.

In the history of humanity, the emotional has never been prioritized like it is in today's society.

Follow your heart, let emotions flow, don't hold them back! Feel free!

The interesting thing about this is that part of it is true, if you retain your emotions you are going to do immense damage to yourself that can even lead not only to illnesses of the soul but also to physical illnesses. But as they always say, "Your rights end where mine begin."

This emotional freedom has made people feel free to be despotic and without any kind of filter, it has turned people into walking time bombs who do not know how to control their emotions and in a moment of tension they explode regardless of the consequences.

This liberation has created such sensitive people who have been called the "glass generation" with whom one must be very delicate because everything offends them.

A few weeks ago I said in one of my Facebook posts that I worked in a department of a university institute where I had to deal with practically all the students of the institution, and on one occasion I said to a student "Wait a moment MIJA" and When I said that word (MIJA) the girl started fighting with me because I called her "mija".

After a while of the girl insulting me, I asked her: Are you from this region of the country? Her answer was "NO" then I asked her: Do you know what the word mija means?

And she answered "NO" so I told her, "And why were you upset when I called you that, if you don't even know what the word means?" At that moment the girl changed her attitude and smiled.

Ladies and gentlemen, I believe that there is no better example of the crystal generation and an Emotionalist society than the one I have just given.

A society where understanding does not matter, where the rational remains in the background and only emotions matter.

And it is impossible for me not to talk about the Lgbtiq+ community or the community "We pass our biology books where the sun does not shine." It is not possible that if I say today that I feel like a girl, I demand that they treat me like a girl, But if tomorrow I wake up feeling like a boy, they must treat me like a boy and if they do, the mess that is formed is big.

¿So what if today I feel like Bill Gates' son? ¿Can I ask the government to demand that Bill Gates give me my share of the inheritance? And don't tell me it's not the same, it's the same logic!

There they do tell me that I must go to science and through the DNA test prove that I really am the son of my daddy Bill, but a man with a beard the length of the Eiffel Tower and with two coconuts in the middle of his legs I must tell him "Juana" because today he woke up feeling like a woman and there it does not matter what his DNA says.

And God forbid don't call him Juana because I am a retrograde, intolerant Christian. And that is another thing, they ask for tolerance, but go to one of their marches so you can see how they ridicule Jesus Christ and play soccer with the Bible. By the way, we Christians are not afraid of anger nor are we intolerant of them, we only say what the Bible and science say.

Sometimes I think, like a conspiracy theorist, that all this has been well planned even by governments and institutions, because an Emotionalist society is also a manipulable society.

And if the church becomes contaminated by that Emotionalist society and becomes an Emotionalist church, then the church will also be a manipulable church and that is what we will talk about in the following chapters.

CHAPTER 4
Emotions and Christianity.

As we have already explained previously, emotions and Christianity are not divorced, they have a marriage, but with conditions, non-negotiable conditions.

We explained that the Bible shows that God is a God with emotions and feelings, who manifests anger, love, contentment. We also saw how Jesus and the Holy Spirit also manifested and still manifest emotions.

We saw how in our praise manual, I am referring to the book of psalms, we are urged to praise God by expressing emotions. We also read the recommendations given regarding praise by one of the great theologians and recognized as one of the great men. of God in history, this is John Wesley.

We also said that the Holy Spirit uses our emotions to work in us.

The Holy Spirit operates in the emotions, the emotions move the will, the will is translated into action, action consists of obedience, life change: lasting transformation.

The leader of the Great Revival of the 18th Century in North America, Jonathan Edwards, says in his masterful book The Religious Affections, that "True religion consists chiefly of holy emotions." He calls these emotions "the energetic and intense performances of the will" and then goes on to say:

"When we receive the Holy Spirit, the Scriptures say we are baptized in "the Holy Spirit and fire" (Matthew 3:11). This "fire" represents the holy emotions that the Spirit produces in us causing our hearts to burn within us (Luke 24:32) ... God, who created us, has not only given us emotions, but has also made them very directly the cause of our actions. We do not make decisions or act unless love, hate, desire, hope, fear, or some other emotion influences us. This is true in both secular and spiritual matters. It is the reason why many people hear the word of God speak to them about things of importance infinite—of God and Christ, sin and salvation, heaven and hell—without having any effect on their attitudes or behavior. What they hear simply does not affect them. It does not touch their emotions. I boldly assert that

I will never No spiritual truth changed the behavior or attitude of a person.

*Person without having awakened his emotions. Never did a sinner desire salvation, nor did a Christian wake up from spiritual coldness, without the truth having affected his heart. That's how important emotions are!... It is proven, then, that our emotions are the axis of authentic religion. Love is not just one of the emotions, but the greatest of them, and, so to speak, the source of the others. It is from love that hate arises, hate for things that are contrary to what we love. From a vigorous and affectionate love towards God the other spiritual emotions will be born: hatred for sin, fear of displeasing God, gratitude to God for his goodness, joy in God when we experience his presence, sadness when we feel his absence, hope for a future enjoyment of God, and zeal for the glory of God. In the same way, love for our neighbor will produce in us everything else that we should feel towards him."
(Jonathan Edwards - The Religious Affections)*

**These paragraphs highlighted in bold and italics were taken from the book "Revival and Emotions" from the Revival Diaries website.

We can understand then that there is no antagonism between emotions and Christianity.

The Problem with Emotions and Christianity

The problem of emotions and Christianity begins with a people of God who, for the most part, do not have spiritual discernment and cannot see that someone squirms a little because they already "have the spirit."

I remember being newly arrived in this city and they invited me to a campaign of our Pentecostal brothers and a boy came up to the stage to give a few words and he twisted his head a little and one of the pastors began to shout "There it is, there it is, there There is God" And I said to myself, ¿What if it is a nervous tic?

I know that today there are some currents of Christianity that do not believe that a Christian can become demon-possessed, but I am going to tell about a situation that occurred several years ago in the church that my father pastors. Well, the church is on the ground floor of the house where my parents live, sometimes my father has to attend to some business and doesn't come down to worship on time.

On one of those days when he did not come down early to worship, the service began and since my parents believed in a Pentecostal church when they began to pastor, they maintained several of the things of the Pentecostal church such as "singing choruses."

The praise began, the praise director began to sing choruses and the people began to come forward to "dance" and give them those uhmmm "trances" where they writhe and things like that, and the person who was leading the praise was happy "because the holy spirit was moving.

Suddenly I hear a movement in the central aisle of the church and it is my father, with clothes almost like being at home and a very angry face, he comes to the altar and tells all the musicians and singers "Stop Everything" and begins to rebuke people's demons who were writhing supposedly because the holy spirit was in them. The curious thing about this event is that no one noticed!

Recently I was listening carefully to two of the Christian music groups that are considered very spiritual and anointed by the majority today and I realized how they surround people with a load of sounds to move the emotions and people do not realize it. note. I remember that I gave my opinion in some Christian groups and almost everyone started shouting: ¡Crucify him! Obviously it happens with preachers too, but the strategies are different, but that comes later.

I want to summarize this chapter by repeating that no, of course not, there is no divorce between Christianity and emotions, there is no divorce between God and emotions. The problem is the extremes and a Christian people who the majority do not know how to differentiate between the spiritual and the emotional. Nowadays, Christian music groups that are great manipulators of emotions are considered super-anointed and the same thing happens with preachers.

CHAPTER 5
An Emotional Christianity.

As I expressed in the previous chapter, Christianity is not divorced from emotions, and neither is the Holy Spirit or Jesus. God has emotions, he made us with emotions, even the holy spirit uses them to work in us.

But, but, but unfortunately, we have a church that for the most part has become emotionalistic, which, as we already explained in chapter one, when emotions are prioritized. A church that loves to be moved by emotions. And as long as there is demand there will be supply.

A church that, for the most part, loves to have a pastor who tells jokes, anecdotes, and makes them laugh. Once I started watching a sermon, it was the first time I was going to hear that pastor preach and I was very expectant, and when that pastor began to speak the first thing he said was: "As always I am going to start with a joke." I said to myself "Whaaaaat?"

And sometimes the reasons those pastors give for doing that seem so coherent. A pastor said that people spent the whole week in stress and strong situations so that they come to church and what they hear are strong words. The truth is that it seems so coherent and logical, but the truth is it is very unbiblical.

For a long time I had that struggle in my mind because the truth is that having a horrible week, one is not going to want a sermon where they feel like they are being beaten to a pulp. After several years of asking myself that question, I discovered that true preaching needs to bother people. who are comfortable and encourage those who are down.

We have a modern church whose goal is emotional. They find out what people like and they give that. And to do this they have had no problems in taking strategies from the world, because as I heard a Christian coach say "We can't be so religious, they are strategies that the world has and they work, so why not use them?"

A church that knows that people like positions, then we see churches with a structure where anyone can be an elder or pastor, they have a promotion structure where the calling of God does not matter, what matters is filling the emotional needs of the people to Thus, having large ministries, which in the end is what matters.

We see a church using all kinds of strategies and even psychological manipulation to achieve its objectives. They have the appearance of spirituality, they disguise themselves as angels of light, but all the strategies they use are carnal.

Someone told me regarding one of the most heretical ministries in my country: "But they have morning prayer sessions every day." Sometimes it is difficult to understand that not everyone who prays is right with God. One of the churches where I have seen the most prayer in my entire country is the same one where I have seen the most evil and injustice. You can read my book "Skeletons in the Closet: Memoirs of a Pastor's Son" for more details.

Today pastors are not preachers, they are Coaches. I don't know if you know, but coaching does not put Christ first, it puts man, and they released a "Christian Coaching" where that reality does not change. The idea is to make us feel good and every Sunday give ourselves an emotional release, where we leave Emotionally Satisfied.

The church adopted psychological strategies from this world and from the moment you enter most churches you have an atmosphere that pleases your flesh, darkness, so that new visitors do not feel intimidated when others see you, disco-style lighting games so that they They sit in a familiar environment, that is, a nightclub, then we have some people with jeans, tennis shoes and not too formal clothes.

A coaching-type preaching focused on men where there is no talk of sin or hell or damnation or anything like that to not cause rejection. Pastor Juan Manuel Vaz said "A Church Restaurant"

And the message that these churches send to those that have not yet modernized is "Adapt or you will disappear." That is why we see today pastors who used to be very radical with the holy, already buying their tennis shoes and jeans to preach on Sundays, buying their games of lights and placing the altar with tables and furniture as if it were the living room of their house and having cool meetings for the young people.

Welcome to the modern church, an emotionalist church that adapts every strategy in the world to it, a church focused on man and his emotions.

And the verse that we should not adapt to the world? That verse doesn't matter, the only thing that matters is filling the church and if we have to put the little sisters in bikinis to achieve this, then it will be done.

Unfortunately, what I expressed in the last paragraph is not an assumption but a truth. A few years ago I was invited to an activity that a church had to attract young people and the activity was a swimming pool, with the little sisters in bathing suits.

An emotionalist church without discernment, which tells you that God is there to make you rich and fulfill all your dreams, a church that is based on cool slogans, but that does not give weight to hell because, in fact, they work for hell, no. They are churches, they are synagogues of Satan.

CHAPTER 6

Great Preachers and Worshipers or Great Manipulators of Emotions.

Today's Christian preachers and singers have specialized in only manipulating emotions.

I saw a video of a pastor who left that world of manipulation and he said: "It's quite easy, I saw a woman sitting alone, but a wedding ring and then I said "The Lord is revealing to me that there is a woman here who "Your husband is unconverted, or has long strayed from the ways of God, the Lord tells you that he has collected each of your tears and that that husband will soon return."

He also said that with young people it was quite easy, he just looked at the one who looked the most excited and said, "The Lord tells you that no one should take your youth for granted, that he would take you to the nations."

You just have to observe and then say the right words with enough emotional charge and people fall flat.

Before continuing, I want to mention something, gentlemen, ladies, understand this, even in any group of 30 or 50 people, there will always be someone who has problems with their parents or problems with their partner, money problems, problems with their boss. If a "minister" comes and says "God shows me that here is a woman named Mary who has problems with her husband, God has this word for you…" I think that for every 100 people at least 3 are called Mary, and as I said in every group, there will always be someone who had or has problems with their parents or with their husband or has financial problems. Honestly, sometimes we are fooled by stupid people.

A person who for years was a worship director (@euthymialy) commented on TikTok that she measures her success according to people's emotional response. She says that perhaps there were services where she went out of tune or got lost in the chords, but she did see an emotional response. of the people she considered that her direction of the praise had been successful, that her direction had been "anointed" but if there were meetings where she did not have a good emotional response from the people, who remained standing without raising their hands, she considered that There was a spiritual oppression in the environment and then over time she learned what chords to play, what words to say to achieve an emotional response from people and that at that time she believed that this was being guided by the spirit, but today she understands which was emotional manipulation.

I also had a very direct experience regarding praise, a young musician and singer who had recently arrived at the church told me that he did not need to pray a lot to lead the praise services, that the secret was saying the right words at the right time. and he could make people cry in the middle of worship.

The sad thing about this story is that it was true, a few weeks later they had him lead a Sunday service and I had a double surprise, the first surprise was that he could actually do it, the second surprise was that no one noticed.

The other thing that happened was that he wanted to warn and after a few days the whole church was saying that what I was envious of him was because he had more anointing than me. You can read the full story in my book Skeletons in the Closet, I don't want to go into too much detail here.

Going back to pastors, evangelists, prophets and others, I have seen so many things that it is painful to write them down. But as for the prophets and evangelists, it is so sad that today they care about money. A few years ago an evangelist came to the city and was invited to a church and said that God had that church as the spearhead in the city and so he went to all the churches in the city saying the same thing to ensure good offerings.

I think one of the things that gave me the most pain was with a pastor who an evangelist prophesied that he would have a church with 5 thousand people, when that pastor had never exceeded 200 or 300 people and that pastor even prostituted the gospel with so much as having his 5000 and his 5000 never arrived and currently that pastor even departed from the ways of God.

They are evil people who only say what they know people want to hear, and they know that people will fill their pockets with offerings if they say nice things.

But really not all people are victims, we know that Jesus said that false prophets would deceive many (Matthew 24:11) but the Bible also tells us that there will be people looking for teachers who will tell them what they want to hear (2 Timothy 4:3)

In my life in the church I have seen many forms of emotional manipulation from pastors. From affirmation, to flattery, which by the way is one of the best forms of manipulation, and intimidation, where they scare people with curses. I know people who have seen pastors do horrible things and have never said anything, but continue to idolatrously support the pastor because of all the intimidating preachings they have heard, starting with the simplest and most effective, that of David and Saul.

If with the preaching of David and Saul they do not get the church to allow them to do ANYTHING, in addition to blind obedience, there they go with a little stronger preaching where they clarify to the people that they do not want to scare them or that they are cursing them , who only want to free them from evil.

Remember, a manipulator will never say "Hello, good morning, I am a manipulative pastor, nice to meet you." Someone said that pride can be disguised in many ways, even humility.

The Bible says that Satan disguises himself as an angel of light, he does not appear and say "hello, I am the devil, be afraid of me" Nooooo!!! You know, the most heretical churches I know in my country are where they seem to love people the most. In those churches I have seen people treated with so much love that not even God reaches them.

Sometimes we forget that these people are experts in manipulation, they do not leave anything to "luck" but they study how they should speak, how they should walk, how they should smile, how their face should look, how to pronounce each word, what words say and which ones don't... They are experts! They live perfecting their "Art"

They know exactly the words they must say to win you over, they know what this emotionalist society likes and they know that emotionalism is within the church and they know that almost no one has discernment and that if they do things well they will have a lot of idolaters. that they are going to blindly obey what they say and they are going to defend them to the death even if they see them do the most vile things and that they are never going to check the Bible to see if something it says is correct biblically speaking. This is how delicate this is!

As far as praise goes, I think I'm understating it if I say it's HORRIFYING, a bunch of showrunners and emotion manipulators being recognized as anointed worshippers. They surround you in sound, a lot of noise, a little blah, blah, here and there, they push the emotional buttons that they know move you and you already come out saying that they are the most anointed Christian music group that has ever existed.

Aside from music and pastors, there is another area where I have seen horrific emotional manipulation is in gospel groups. Previously, I belonged to a ministry whose focus is evangelism above everything else and there they had a person who surpassed everyone in terms of manipulation.

First, well-prepared plays to move the emotions, at the end, he would come to the front, well-prepared music would be played to continue the work of emotional manipulation that had begun with the plays, he would ask that people close their eyes. eyes with the same idea that everyone does, it is easier for the music to do its job if they have their eyes closed, then he proceeded to change his tone of voice and began with the phrase "If you want to cry, cry",

After a few moments He said "I know you want to cry" after repeating those two phrases several times, interspersing some phrases where he made people understand why they should cry, he achieved his goal and then it was even easier to make them come forward "to receive Jesus" or that from where they were they would repeat "the prayer of faith"

Others, when "making the call to repent" only said the phrase "How many want to be blessed?" I assure you that they did not say anything else, they only asked people that question, and they told them "If you want to be blessed, raise your hand and repeat this prayer."

I don't know if I should explain why that is emotional manipulation, but maybe there is someone who doesn't notice it. If you ask me if I want money no matter how spiritual I claim to be, I will say yes, if you ask me what or any Christian if I want to be blessed, no matter how clear I am that spiritual It is more important, no matter how regenerated and separated from the world I am, I am going to respond that I do want to be blessed.

Now think about the response you will receive from an unregenerate person, who lives not for God but for his flesh, when you ask him if he wants to be blessed.

Others, to create empathy while evangelizing, say "I am just like you." Once I went out to evangelize with a group of boys, and a young man said this phrase and I was waiting for him to add more, because if you tell a non-Christian that you are just like him, ¿then why will he receive Christ? I asked and the answer they gave me was that, that it was only to create empathy.

Writing about that, something comes to mind that is very fashionable these days, and that is to say while making the call "Do not think that the church is full of Saints, not the church is full of sinners." At first it seems coherent. and logical, but really? Full?! Beloved, if the church you attend is FULL of sinners, there is a problem. ¿I understand that sanctification is a process and we will be perfected until Christ comes, but IS IT FULL? Without a doubt that is another phrase to create empathy.

Today the most effective evangelism strategy is to believe people that their sin is not that serious, I have actually seen models of evangelism where the word sin is not mentioned, they are implicitly prohibited from telling people that they are sinners because that is offensive.

I managed to study the evangelism methods of the largest ministries in my country and I was able to understand why they are the largest ministries. Not because they are the most spiritual, but because of the number of psychological manipulation tools they use to gain membership.

1 Timothy 2:4 But as we were approved by God to be entrusted with the gospel, so we speak; not as to please men, but God, who tests our hearts.

Romans 16:18 For such people do not serve our Lord Jesus Christ, but their own bellies, and with smooth words and flattery they deceive the hearts of the naive.

1 Corinthians 2:4 And my speech and my preaching were not with persuasive words of human wisdom, but in demonstration of the Spirit and power,

1 Corinthians 2:13 Which also we speak, not in words taught by human wisdom, but in those taught by the Spirit, adjusting the spiritual to the spiritual.

Colossians 2:4 And I say this so that no one deceives you with persuasive words.

I think from the verses above we can see that the apostle Paul did not need manipulation or persuasion techniques. The problem is that at one point many realized that they could obtain "the same results" using human wisdom, but with persuasion, manipulation and human wisdom they can never be the same results, because a place full of people is not the same as a place full of people. a place full of saved people, which can genuinely be called Church.

CHAPTER 7

Ingredients Necessary to be Manipulated.

Not only is a manipulator necessary, it is necessary for the "victim" to have the right characteristics.

One of the characteristics of a person with emotional intelligence is that he is able to recognize and control his feelings and has self-esteem.

This is important because if a person does not have self-esteem, the manipulator will take advantage of this and use words of affirmation, motivation and even flattery in order to create dependency and have control of the person.

In the same way, a person who does not have well defined and valued emotions and does not have rational control of them, which is another of the characteristics of an emotionally intelligent person, is an easy victim to be manipulated.

Today's society has been guided to follow their heart, to let their emotions direct them and by teaching them to leave emotions uncontrolled they make people easily manipulated.

Another important thing is the affective and emotional deficiencies that a person may have. Where there are emotional deficiencies there is a potential victim for a manipulator.

I remember having a very pretty student, but her husband told her that she was ugly and that no one was going to love her like that, and the young woman put up with all kinds of abuse from that man because that man took advantage of her lack of self-esteem to make her believe that she was ugly and no one else would love her.

I knew a person who manipulated others just by flattering them. We must recognize that every human being has basic emotional needs such as love, affirmation, respect. And manipulators, whether you are Christians or not, are specialists in exploiting those emotional needs; That is why one of the characteristics of emotionally intelligent people is important, which is rational control of emotions.

Depending on the type of life we have had, we will all have a greater or lesser need for affection. A person lacking affection can easily be detected by a manipulator and make that person lacking affection their victim, obviously this applies inside and outside the church.

I met a woman in a church whose father abandoned her when she was very young and the pastor knew her story and used the woman's need for paternal love to tell her to take him as her father. The pastor began to work on her with affection, filling the void of affection that she needed to such an extent that she became a blind follower of him.

Over the years I could see how the pastor did all kinds of tricks, injustices, evil... in front of her and she never said a single word, but rather continued to follow him idolatrically.

Another human need widely exploited by manipulators is the need for recognition, which is why many churches have hundreds of levels of leadership. Giving someone a title or position is a good strategy to keep them in a church no matter how heretical it may be.

In many companies and churches, when they know that someone knows a lot of company secrets, the way to keep them quiet is to give them a boss position, even if they are the most incapable person in the world.

One man said "If we don't study the scriptures, we will be slaves to whatever sounds nice." That's why it's easy to understand why those manipulators attack those who study the Bible so much. I know of a pastor who mocks from the pulpit calling them "Bibliolocos" and no pastor finds a church that studies the Bible manipulative or that is like the brothers of Berea who when they get home they check to see if everything they They told them it's true.

These types of people, if they come to give Bible studies, it is more than anything so that they do not criticize them, they try to interpret the Bible to people in a way to make the Bible say what they want it to say.

CHAPTER 8

How to Avoid Being a Victim of Emotional Manipulation in the Church.

I have been studying for years how manipulators work in the church, both in worship and in the pastorate, but if I give you a human strategy to avoid being a victim of manipulators I am not doing anything, so my main advice is to have total dependence on the Holy Spirit. We must also have discernment, we must ask for it, we must beg for it because we are in a time where manipulators of all kinds are going to arise.

We must be people who depend on the scriptures above all else. I have had to see pastors that I love the way they speak, my flesh loves what they say, I love the way they are, but when I filter what they say through the Bible and see that they are manipulative heretics, with great pain I discard them.

Of course one of the main things is what we said in chapter 1, we should not give priority to emotions, in short we should not be emotionalists.

We must be careful with our emotional deficiencies because these people are experts in recognizing our emotional deficiencies and they go straight to making up for them in order to manipulate us.

Please be careful with people who seem to have too much love, we measure someone's spirituality first by what he believes, if his doctrine is biblical.

Sometimes I see Christians as a teenage girl who falls in love with anyone who says three nice words to her. A mature Christian is not going to go after a pastor who tells him three nice things, a mature Christian is going to biblically evaluate every word the pastor says no matter how much he loves him and no matter how much he believes that he is a man of God.

Beloved, there are people who think that faith and the use of the brain do not connect, but look at what these verses say:

1 Corinthians 14:15 What then? I will pray with the spirit, but I will also pray with the understanding; I will sing with the spirit, but I will also sing with the understanding.

That verse made me remember a song that began to be sung in all the churches in my country and people were inspired by singing it and without analyzing much I said to myself, How is it that the glory of God comes out to play and lets me win?

Another very famous song ♫♪Remove my stone today, call me by name♪♫ I told myself! But on the quote that the song is based on (John 11:38-44) Jesus did not remove the stone, Jesus ordered others to move it.

And if we talk about the song "the Shunammite" Ah well! I have tried to believe that in some parts they were too creative, I have looked for a thousand ways to excuse those who wrote it, ¡but oh no! However, that was another song that was sung as if it were the national anthem.

And I'm only mentioning two, but there are many more songs with questionable lyrics and that we don't love just because they sound nice and because they make us happy or make us cry.

And we get used to that, that it sounds beautiful and that it moves the emotions regardless of whether what it says is biblical or not, what matters is that it sounds beautiful and that it moves my emotions and the same thing happens with the sermons.

If they sound nice and made me feel something nice, I'm going to say that it was a tremendous preaching, even if the preacher said that Plunder was called that because he was a looter.

Mark 12:33 And to love Him with all your heart, with all your understanding, with all your soul, and with all your strength, and to love your neighbor as yourself, is more than all burnt offerings and sacrifices. Tremendous that we are still asked to love him with understanding.

ANNEXES

45

What does the Bible say about managing/controlling emotions?

What would we humans be like if we never got excited, if we were able to control our emotions at all times? Perhaps we would become like robots, responding to all situations with logic and never with emotions. But God created us in his image, and God's emotions are revealed in the scriptures; Therefore, God created us emotional beings.

We feel love, joy, happiness, guilt, anger, disappointment, fear, etc. Sometimes our emotions are pleasant experiences, and sometimes they are not. Sometimes our emotions are founded on truth, and sometimes they are "false" because they are based on erroneous premises. For example, if we falsely believe that God is not in control of the circumstances of our lives, we may experience the emotions of fear, despair, or anger based on that false belief. Regardless, emotions are powerful and real to the one who is feeling them.

That being said, it is important that we learn about managing emotions, rather than allowing our emotions to manage us. For example, when we feel angry, it is important to be able to stop, identify that we are angry, examine our hearts to determine why we are angry, and then proceed in a biblical way.

Emotions that are out of control do not usually produce God-honoring results: "For the anger of man does not work the righteousness of God" (James 1:20).

Our emotions, like our minds and bodies, are greatly influenced by humanity's fall into sin. In other words, our emotions are tainted by our sinful nature, and that is why we need to control them. The Bible tells us that we have to be controlled by the Holy Spirit (Romans 6; Ephesians 5:15-18; 1 Peter 5:6-11), and not by our emotions. If we acknowledge our emotions and bring them before God, then we can present our hearts to Him and allow Him to do His work in our hearts and direct our actions.

Sometimes this can simply mean that God comforts us, reassures us, and reminds us not to fear. Other times, He may lead us to forgive or ask for forgiveness.

The Psalms are an excellent example of managing emotions and how to bring our emotions to God. Many Psalms are filled with raw emotions, but these are poured out before God in an attempt to seek truth and justice from him.

Sharing our feelings with other people is also useful for managing emotions. The Christian life is not supposed to be lived alone. God has given us the gift of other believers who can share our burdens and whose burdens we also share (Romans 12; Galatians 6:1-10; 2 Corinthians 1:3-5; Hebrews 3:13).

Other believers can also remind us of God's truth and offer us a new perspective. When we feel discouraged or fearful, we can benefit from the encouragement, exhortation, and reassurance that other believers offer us. Often when we encourage others, we ourselves are encouraged.

Likewise, when we feel joy, it usually increases when we share it.

Allowing our emotions to control us is not at all pious, nor is denying or censoring our emotions. We must thank God for our ability to feel emotion and manage our emotions as a gift from Him. The way we manage our emotions is through our growth in our walk with God. We are transformed by the renewing of our minds (Romans 12:1-2) and the power of the Holy Spirit, which produces self-control in us (Galatians 5:22-23). We need a daily boost of biblical principles, a desire to grow in the knowledge of God and spend time meditating on the attributes of God.

We should try to know more about God and share more of our hearts with God through prayer. Christian fellowship is another important part of spiritual growth.

https://www.gotquestions.org/Espanol/manejo-emociones.html

How to use the Bible to manipulate people?

Preachers today have become sort of mega stars and influencers within the Christian community.

Many of them use their preaching skills to persuade weak minds and turn them into a gold mine and their staunchest fans.

But the saddest thing is not the misuse that is being given to the preaching of the gospel today, but rather seeing Christians unable to notice a wolf in sheep's clothing that is "preaching" in front of them.

My heart fills with sadness when I observe "hypnotized" Christians shouting Amen to any type of thing a preacher says without even analyzing whether what he said has biblical support.

We assume that since a preacher is used by God, whatever comes out of his mouth is what God wants us to hear. However, we forget that he (preacher) is a person who can make mistakes and twist his heart from the right path and become a thief with Bible in hand.

The Marjoe Gortner documentary

A few days ago I came across a video on the Internet that told about the amazing revelations that the famous "evangelist" Marjoe Gortner had made.

An American preacher who, after having been involved in the ministry since his childhood, ended up confessing through a documentary that he never believed in God, and that everything he did was more false than the vitamins in a McDonald's hamburger.

Whoever serves God for money,

he is capable of serving the devil
for a better salary.
—Charles Spurgeon

In this documentary, Gortner confesses how he used suggestion to hypnotize Christians into believing that God worked great miracles through him, and that he was truly an anointed man of Jehovah.

The reason? Fill his pockets with money to satisfy all the pleasures that he gave himself during his life.

In this documentary titled Marjoe, you can see the unscrupulous strategies that this man used to live off his false facade as a man used by God.

You will wonder: Why was no one able to stop him? Because in his time what happens in our times happened:

Christians lulled by the lies of false preachers who do not seek truth or discernment. You. 4:6

So it came to pass that this wicked man used the media to make fools of God's people.

You can imagine the amount of comments and ridicule that this documentary will have generated at the time.

The problem is not just money When I mention that the preaching of the gospel has become the laughingstock of the world, I am not only referring to the vile use of enriching that many "preachers" use, but also to the fallacies with which they have been built many denominations.

Apparently anyone in his free time has the fascinating idea of being a preacher and starts talking about anything that comes to mind without even doing a deep study of the Bible.

Other people, who heard a very famous preacher and loved what he said, begin to copy and preach the same thing without realizing the horrors into which they are falling. But there were also false prophets among the people, just as there will be false teachers among you, who will covertly introduce destructive heresies.

Unfortunately we live in a time when it seems that Christians are too lazy to open their Bibles to check whether what is said is true or not. We are quickly persuaded by well-spoken preaching and ignore the truth of the scriptures.

Pastors can spend years twisting the Scriptures but no one is able to be reasonable, open their Bible, and begin to analyze whether what their pastor said is a biblical message or not.

I already told you at the beginning of this article, a pastor is also a person who makes mistakes and whose heart is capable of being twisted. Many preachers may not live with a crooked heart far from God, but in their biblical ignorance they make serious mistakes and in the same way guide their congregation like a ship adrift.

Sensible and rational Christians It is very sad that in the 21st century, Christians have fallen into the traps of characters who easily sweeten our ears and without realizing it, lead us little by little towards the abyss.

We have turned the gospel into an emotional fad by letting ourselves be blindly guided by people who don't even know the direction they are going.

Today's Christians are no longer sensible or rational. They allow themselves to be persuaded very easily, falling into deception due to the bad habit of not reading or meditating personally on the Word of God. Each denomination has its own interpretation of the Bible. They unite thoughts and ideas in order to build a doctrine with which all members of the church will identify.

But on many occasions these doctrines are full of fallacies that ironically believers applaud and accept as absolute truth.

I remember visiting Sunday school at my friend Omar's church and hearing the teacher say something that completely shocked me. He said that the Holy Spirit is not enough for the growth of a Christian, professional and economic growth is also necessary.

At that moment I wanted to stand up and face this teacher whose teaching many Christians unfortunately applauded and supported with an Amen. But this is not the only case. I could list many others in which pastors, leaders, teachers, etc., have said egregious things and the congregation in unison said Amen!

It seems that Christians forgot that God created them by giving them the rational capacity that distinguishes them from animals to think, understand and evaluate. In Mt. 22:37 we can observe how Jesus teaches his disciples to love God with all of his mind.

In other words, Jesus is telling his disciples that they must be sensible and rational in living for God by behaving according to common sense and not getting carried away by uncontrollable emotions. Guilty for allowing themselves to be persuaded While it is true that those who mislead the congregation into blunders will have their pay, those who allow themselves to be mistaught will also have their share of lamentation and gnashing of teeth.

Because you are also partly to blame for the fact that there are preachers, leaders, teachers, etc., who are leading the congregation badly. You have total access to the Bible in your hands and you are not able to take a little of your time and begin to analyze everything that your pastor has said or the preaching of the one you constantly listen to.

Therefore, you will also have to answer for not knowing how to examine everything, retain the good and reject the bad (1 Thes. 5:21).

Human beings by nature are easy to persuade. This is a double tool that big brands take advantage of when offering us a product for sale. The same thing happens with Christians when listening to a teaching or preaching. They act motivated by their emotions and not by the irrefutable truth of the Word of God.

They allow themselves to be persuaded by well-spoken preachings and doctrines that lull them to sleep, completely ignoring everything that happens in front of their noses. And perhaps you will say that it is not your fault that there are lying and swindling preachers.

But you are to blame for not opening your eyes and mind to see the evil path they are leading you on. Or did they perhaps plant a chip in your brain with which it is impossible for you to be rational?

Not true.

Nobody, I believe, planted a chip in the brains of the parishioners of the Light of the World sect to worship Samuel Joaquín Flores and Naasón Joaquín García like a god.

Cash Luna, Guillermo Maldonado, Ana Méndez, and others do not have the absolute power to prevent you from being rational and sensible.

The power to choose was placed upon you by God the moment you were created. Don't come up with excuses that these characters are the ones who tricked you.

Lastly, I am sad to see what the gospel of God has become today. I think the formula has changed from "I am not ashamed of the gospel" to "the gospel is ashamed of me."

We live in times when the gospel is synonymous with stupidity, poor minds, and people who are easy to manipulate. Without realizing it, we Christians have ended up giving reason for the world to think that Jesus Christ is a mere formula to dominate the masses and make a few extra dollars for ourselves.

But it's never late. We can still rectify every mistake we have made as a church. We can still return to the pure and true gospel without being moved by emotions by being sensible and rational.

Start today with this change. Open your Bible the same times—or more—as you open your Facebook. Study the Bible as many times—or more—as you do your best math book.

Retain everything the pastor, preacher, or teacher says. Take it home and analyze it with the help of the Holy Spirit. If you do not have a large library with tools to do an in-depth study, these 5 online Christian resources to study the Bible will be a very powerful help for you.

Remember that the gospel is walked with faith, but a faith that is rational that takes you along the paths of common sense and offers you salvation instead of manipulation.

Max Damián

https://www.maxdamian.com/search/label/Vida

FINAL WORDS

Jesus loved his enemies, but he insulted those who distorted the gospel in many ways. By this what I mean is that the fact that in this book I expose the manipulation tools of false teachers does not mean that I do not love the church, it only means that I truly love the church and those wolves are not true pastors and those churches are not true churches but synagogues of satan.

My precious ones, please beware of those bitches, beware of those dogs, those who seem so loving do not want to win you for Christ, they want to win you for themselves.

Please beware of those who talk too nice. Beware of those people who have an appearance of humility, learn to discern, to go beyond appearances.

Please, none of this means that you should be cold, or act like the young man I told about who came to visit us.

Please, if you have any questions, contact me through the contact information that appears on my personal blog or on any of my book blogs. I love the church, I love the body of Christ, I will answer all your questions and help you in any way I can.

Please read my other books, they are all written to bless the body of Christ.

I send you all lots of kisses!

I am elprofebubba

gonzalezdomingo@gmail.com

https://elprofebubba.blogspot.com

https://bookskeletonsinthecloset.blogspot.com/

https://bookadifferentkindofglory.blogspot.com/

https://bookmyjourneydiscoveringthegospel.blogspot.com/

https://elprofebubba.blogspot.com

Also by Domingo González Jr.

Cristianismo en Medio De una Sociedad Emocionalista
Christianity in the Midst of an Emotionalist Society
Cristianismo No Meio de uma Sciedade Emocionalista